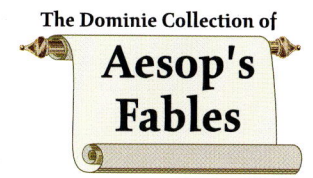

The Dominie Collection of Aesop's Fables

The Miller Who Tried to Please Everyone

Retold by Alan Trussell-Cullen

Illustrated by David Preston Smith

Dominie Press, Inc.

Once there was a miller who spent his days grinding grain into flour.

He had a donkey that was too old and too tired to work anymore. So the miller and his young son decided to take the donkey to town and sell him at the market.

It was a hot, sunny day as all three set out along the dusty road. The miller led the donkey, and his son walked beside him.

Soon they met a group of young girls gossiping on the roadside. When the girls saw them approaching, they began to point and laugh.

"What fools they are!" the girls said. "There they are, walking along a hot, dusty road when one of them could be riding on their donkey."

"They must be right," thought the miller. So he sat his son on the donkey and they continued on their way to town.

Soon they came upon a group of old men gossiping on the roadside.

"Look at that!" the old men said, looking very shocked. "That poor old man has to walk while his strong young boy gets to ride. The old man should be the one riding, not the young boy!"

"They must be right," thought the miller. So he lifted his son off the donkey's back and climbed on the animal himself. They continued on their way, with the miller on the donkey and the young boy walking alongside.

Soon they came upon a group of women gossiping on the roadside.

"Look at that!" the women said, looking very shocked. "That cruel old man is riding the donkey while his poor little boy has to walk!"

"They must be right," thought the miller. So he reached down and picked up his little boy and sat him down in front of him on the donkey. Then they continued on their way to town.

As they came nearer to the town, they met a farmer taking his goat to the market.

"Surely that isn't your own poor donkey!" the farmer said.

"Why yes, it is," said the miller.

"I would never have believed it," said the farmer. "Imagine making a poor old animal carry two people on a hot day like today. The poor creature looks worn out. It would be better if you carried him, rather than making him carry you."

"He must be right," thought the miller. So he and his son climbed off the donkey. They tied the donkey's legs together with rope and slung him over a pole. The miller and his son put the pole on their shoulders and began to walk across the bridge that led into the town.

The townsfolk saw them coming. "What a ridiculous sight!" they said. And they all began to laugh.

The donkey was frightened by all the noise and began to wriggle and kick. Suddenly, the ropes around his legs snapped, and he tumbled off the pole and into the river.

Several minutes passed, and the donkey jumped out onto the bank and ran away. He was feeling happy and refreshed after his swim in the cool water.

The miller and his son had to turn around and walk all the way home again.

"At least we learned one thing," said the miller as they plodded back along the hot, dusty road.

"When you try to please everyone, you end up pleasing no one."